THE SOFTNESS UNDER THE SCARS

A COLLECTION OF PRIVATE AND NOT SO PRIVATE OF LYRICS, POEMS & THOUGHTS

FRANKI OLINGER

ISBN: 979-8-9850220-6-3

Printed in the United States of America

Olinger Coaching & Consulting
www.olingercoaching.com

DEDICATION

This book is dedicated to my grandchildren Avery, Adaline and Killian. May you always know how much I love you with all of my heart and soul.

And after I am on to the next adventure of life, I hope these words will be a friend to you in my absence.

I never even pretended to be perfect, so the words in this book may not be what you'd expect. But if you're my grandchildren, chances are - you'll identify in one way or another... sorry about that. But every human has a dark side and a light side. To deny this is in error.

Always be mindful of the feelings of those around you.

Always be authentically you.

Always remember, you are loved and adored.

(p.s. I left you some final words at the back of this book)

Love you,
  Your Babushka

ACKNOWLEDEGMENTS

I would like to acknowledge and thank the following people. Without your help, this book would not have come to fruition and I would not be who I am.

God, Source, Universe... whatever you want to be called. First and foremost, thank you for my life, talents and soul.
Jenson Olinger, my husband and biggest supporter. You make being your wife and partner so incredibly easy. James Merendino, my friend. Thank you for writing the foreword to this book for me. Your talent and friendship are beyond measure. My children Bryanna, Kirsten, Corey & Gunnar. You have all healed me in your own special way. Gene Louis, for your collaboration on Bonnie & Clyde. Andy McCarty, for giving me the one line in Song For The Devil that I just couldn't find for myself. Alex Smith, you are still one of my favorite people and I miss our days on stage together. Chris Khaos (Spohr), your screaming in the back ups made some of the songs what they were. I also miss sharing a stage with you. My Wildbunch friends... you know who you are and there are WAYYYY too many of you to name. My Tribe of Elephants, my soul family. Brian Lavin, you have always supported me in whatever I have ever done since the day we became friends. I'd say I love you but that weirds you out. Don-e, Shawn Noon, Joey Ruffino... I miss being called Sarge and I am forever grateful for your encouragement to me to sing and be unafraid (do you regret it now? Haha) Don Jose Ruiz, mi hermano, my brother, my friend. Thank you for always encouraging me to embrace myself and share of myself freely. My mom, for passing down the gift of words to me. And finally, my dad... Larry Howitt. Your blood runs through my veins and your spirit in my soul. I am your child and for this I am most grateful. I love you Daddy.

"I don't care if I come across beautiful, or ugly. As long as I present myself authentically - I will not feel shame..."

Franki Olinger

FOREWORD

As a filmmaker who's work skews darkly humorous, my understanding of life is somewhat distorted and often cynical. So, when I come across an author who genuinely is able to shrug off the absurdity of the human experience and extrapolate meaning, I take notice.

Unfortunately, this doesn't happen very often. It's much easier to wallow in empty existentialism than to risk searching one's soul and coming up with answers to very difficult questions. Franki Olinger is one such author.

Having known Franki for many for years, I have had the pleasure to witness her evolve as a person and an artist.

Her ability to see life through the lens of pain and somehow turn it into beauty is astonishing. Her journey has been a spiritual pursuit and her thirst for understanding is unquenchable. That coupled with raw talent and wisdom, Franki has put together a collection of writings that capture this personal growth with a confident and unique voice.

What impresses me about this collection of prose, is the mixture of lyrical language, brutal honesty and rough frankness. There is no filter at all. Each piece either warms you like a soothing bath or hits you like a sledgehammer. She presents parts of herself and her life, the good with the cataclysmic, and serves it with a healthy dose of compassion.

By the end you find yourself understood. As if Franki is your friend who would not, could not judge. This book is an invitation to a place that feels like home.

James Merendino -
Filmmaker

PREFACE

May the words in this book become a blanket for your soul and a mirror for your heart.

Since I was a little girl, I've always written my thoughts down. Good and bad. Weird and beautiful. Whether on napkins, notepads, leaves... really anything I could find to write on - wherever I was - I was writing down whatever was in my head.

I am an outwardly positive person, just ask anyone who truly knows me. But I am also a human, and every once in a while I feel a reminder that there is a darkness inside. I don't judge what I'm writing down. Ugly, beautiful, I've always written all of it without a filter.

And if I'm being honest, I feel as though I have many different and sometimes opposing points of view, all living harmoniously inside my mind. I honor all of the feelings I live with inside.

But when I feel inspired, or emotional... different personas pick up the pen to write. Franki Doll, my alter-ego is angry and combative when she writes.

Franki Olinger, the spiritual teacher writes with love and compassion.
Little Franki, the child within writes with confusion and pain...
And there are many more who will have their say as well.
I let them all have their say - authentically.

There are way too many things I've written to put into this book. So I chose some at random to share here. Judge or embrace my thoughts as you wish. My hope is that you may find some comfort, some inspiration, or maybe not feel as alone after reading this.

And at the very least, there is a record of me to be read when I'm gone.

From my heart to yours, happy reading.

Franki

Read with your heart

Read with your mind

Read with your soul

But Never,

Never,

Read with your ego.

Franki Olinger

1

MY ANONYMOUS FRIENDS

●

Hurt people
hurt people...

But broken people
heal broken people.

2

NOT SUPPOSED TO HAPPEN

♠

I've given up
Trying to fight my love for you
No matter what, I won't say it

Every time I let my guard down
Enough to let you in
Fear jumps in and I can't say it

So here and now
I'll do it just this once, I'll tell you
That I'm no good without you

Don't you know I don't think I'm good enough for anyone
I'll say it loud and clear

I'm not the tough girl I pretend to be inside
I'm not cold and I'm not angry,
That's just where I hide

Cause if you knew you owned my soul
Then you'd know you have control
And this was not supposed to happen

I won't look up
Cause when your blue, meets my green eyes
You won't have to ask for answers

I've tried it all
I leave, I laugh I cry - alone I'll die
There's no such thing as life without you

But still I cannot find
The voice to tell you that I
I've been conquered by you - gently

All I wanted was peace
To heal this wounded heart
Instead I found myself in love

I'm not the tough girl I pretend to be inside
I'm not cold and I'm not angry,
That's just where I hide

Cause if you knew you owned my soul
Then you'd know you have control
And this was not supposed to happen

No this was not supposed to...

3

FORGIVENESS & A SCORECARD

♦

There was a time
That I was a human being
Being human

And I forgot how to forgive
I took score
And everything anyone ever did to me
I made sure I was going to remember

Dear Mom,
Remember when I told you that you were the worst
person on earth? That I never wanted to be like you?
I was wrong.
I understand you now, and I would like nothing more
than to be just like you. You're a good woman with a
good heart.

Dear Dad,
Remember when I told you that you didn't understand
me?
And that I couldn't talk to you sometimes?
I was wrong.
You do understand me. And there's no one on earth
who gives advice quite like you.

There are so many people I have been wrong about.
And I forgot. I forgot how to forgive others.
And I forgot how to forgive myself.

I would do things that hurt me again and again so I could remind myself that I was a bad person.
But I was wrong.

See the second we can forgive others, and ourselves
Our lives become new... our lives become different
Forgiveness is one of the greatest gifts we can give ourselves
... give anyone

And it doesn't cost us anything at all except maybe some EGO
But hasn't that thing gotten us in enough trouble already?
Learn how to forgive. Give it away freely
Remember that we're all in the middle of a lesson here

And if you're standing there with a scorecard
That scorecard is holding you down
You should probably just rip it up
You should probably just throw it away
You know, you should probably just start over

As long as you're still here
It's not too late to forgive anyone for being human
Even if it's just yourself.   ✘

4

FAIRYTALES & NIGHTMARES

💧

What do you want from me
A handout in the night
A kiss a hug - Or do you wanna fight?
Which one of us changed
The answer to your dreams
I never said that I was Mrs. - Right now is the time
This moment is divine
Standing tall we feel the fall - We're lost but we can find
It's not like me to stay
Stuck in this decay
I'm not the kind of girl to try to live this way

Can't you see
I can't breathe
What is it you want for me to be?
Close your eyes
And believe
This isn't just a Fairy Tale to me!

What do I owe you?
These promises were never meant to keep you from the
night
I feel like sleeping
But lie there until dawn - and know this isn't right
I'm stuck in this decay

I cannot live this way
Monotony of all I see - Is truly killing me
And if this is the way
I end it all today
At least it's known that I changed things
That led it all astray

Can't you see
I can't breathe
What is it you want for me to be?
Close your eyes
And believe
This isn't just a Fairy Tale to me!

I will NOT settle down
I wont' be back around
I've stood in line for all this mediocrity I've found
And if there comes a day
I look the other way
And find I'm on the path that led the others all astray
I'll walk with all my might
And I'll make the wrong things right
But I WILL NOT settle down
And I will not SETTLE!

Can't you see
I can't breathe
What is it you want for me to be?
Close your eyes
And believe
This isn't just a Fairy Tale to me!

5

THE SOFTNESS UNDER THE SCARS

I heard a rumor
that someone told you
you were not beautiful
That you were flawed and broken
That your voice didn't matter

I heard a rumor
That you believed what they said
That you entertained this in your head
Until these words became your own truth

I heard a rumor
That you sabotage your life
That you hide now in plain sight
That you have become the character
They've assigned you to be

I heard a rumor
That you know down deep inside
That somethings just not right
And you feel like no one truly knows you

I heard a rumor
That you carry discomfort around
That the mirror reflects someone else
When you look inside your own eyes

I heard a rumor
That you will remember who you are
The softness under your scars
That you'll yearn to be the real you

I heard a rumor that you want to be the real you
But you're scared you'll be rejected
Your heart won't be protected
That you may not be accepted

But I also know the truth
That you present a false identity
And so the real you has already being rejected
Because up front, they have no clue who you are

I heard a rumor
That you only get one life
The one that you're not living
That you've settled on existing

I heard a rumor that you stopped all the hiding
That you're bravely returning to authenticity
The ones who truly know you - love you completely
The Good, the Bad and the ugly

I heard a rumor that you've stopped rejecting yourself
That you put your ego up on a shelf
And you've finally returned to who you are
The softness under your scars.

6

I AM ALIVE

Sometimes I feel
Sometimes I feel all alone
Sitting there all by myself
In my room
In my car
In my head

And I think to myself
Why?
Why do I feel this way?
Why am I forced to feel this way?
Am I a Victim?
Am I a Victim?

Or am I a chooser?
Do I choose to feel this way because inside I really do?
Or because - I don't know how to feel
Because I don't know how to be happy
Because I don't know how to LET myself be happy

Do I not know how to succeed?
Do I not know how to let anyone else succeed?
Have I forgotten what it's like to be a human being?

Or am I being 100 % human... now.
I don't wanna do this
I don't want to be alone
I don't want to feel like I'm all alone
I don't want to stand here any longer
And think to myself
This is the way it's always going to be

I can't have that
I can't feel that
I can't be that
I can't be trapped by those emotions
And so I'm not going to
I choose not to do that anymore
From this moment on, I am reborn.

I am empowered,
I am joyous,
I am free

I am abundant,
I am loved,
I am amazing

And there's nothing that can stand in my way
Except for me

I am alive!
I am alive!

I can feel everything in my soul
Just demanding me to listen

And telling me there's something else
There's something more for us to do ...
There's something more
Something more than this

We were made to create
We were made to be amazing
I was made to stand out in a crowd
And stand up by myself

I was made to be everything I feel inside
From today on, I'm going to do that

This is why

I sit here

And I say these things....

So that maybe you'll do it too.

7

I SAW

I saw you hurt
But cared more about how you hurt me
I saw you need
But cared more about what I needed
I saw you cry
But cared more about you seeing my tears
I saw you shut down
But cared more about not shutting down myself
I saw you plead... with your eyes
But I wished for you to recognize your faults
I saw you pray
But cared more about you worshipping me
I saw you pack
But cared more about the fact you were abandoning me
I saw you leave
And then... I was alone...
It was too late... but I finally saw the problem
I saw myself.

X

8

DO I TRULY KNOW WHAT HUMILITY MEANS

♦

I was born unique.
My DNA proves this.
I am the only version of me that exists.
And.
Every day I am faced with challenges & choices.
I - along with others who have chosen to shine as
bright as they were meant to shine get bullied,
shamed and scorned.

People reject our beauty. They call us arrogant,
egomaniacs, and other assorted names and labels.

This name calling is usually done by people who are
too afraid to follow their own dreams - or people who
are caught up in the mindset or beliefs that some
adult fed to them when they were children.

You see, people are taught to "blend in" - be careful -
don't create too much attention - other people say
things like "who do you think you are to expect
anything more out of life than you were dealt?

They tell you be realistic- work hard for what you get.
Etc. etc. etc. and we buy into this because we don't
want rejection.

But in believing these people, we give up on our dreams or forget we had any dreams altogether.

My favorite thing I hear people say is "STAY HUMBLE" - and many times what that means is "please shrink smaller so that I will feel more comfortable with you" ... But the word humble means "right sized" - "not any more OR ANY LESS" than what you truly are. It takes a brave person to face fear and ridicule to be the best version of themselves that they can be.

People call Ghandi humble - and he was - but can you imagine how hard it must've been for him to step into those shoes with the powers that opposed him?

Whether you are an actor, or artist, or want to be as fit as you can be- it takes humility to do these things. I know I am scared to post these things I write sometimes - my head says "who is going to want to hear a 43 year old tattooed chick preach love and dreams and everything else I teach.

And then this voice - I assume the inner conscious says to me - WHO ARE YOU TO NOT DO THESE THINGS! I didn't make you everything you are so you could hide it! ... I hope those of you who are ready to hear me - hear me. BE YOU. ALL OF YOU. THE BEAUTIFUL - THE UGLY - THE UNIQUE...

When you do this, you tell others that it is ok for them to do the same.

9

I SHOULD BE SLEEPING

Sit in the drive through
The building are crying
The skyline is falling
The smoke starts to fade
One more cigarette
I feel like I'm dying
The angels are crying
It drips off the blade

I scream WHY ME!
Why not
YOU scream
No where does it say...
Life's supposed to go your way...
I scream WHY ME!
Why not
YOU scream
No where does it say...
Life's supposed to go my way...

The Car behind me
Holds 2 blondes in waiting
Too big for mating
Seconds from starving to death
But I'm closing my eyes

The make-up is melting
The drugs are not helping
Fire's consuming

Discomfort is my middle name
One more cigarette
And I feel like I'm...
One more cigarette
Away from...
One More... One More
I should be sleeping at this hour!

10

SAME AS YOU

"So, what race are you?"... he asked, very interested in what my answer would be...

"same as you, I said"...

his eyes grew wide as he looked at the color of his skin compared to mine...

"are you sure?" he asked...

to which I smiled and said "yes, I am most certain"...

he raised his eyebrows and asked me...

"What race do you think that I am?"

with a little laugh... I smiled back and said

"Same as me!"

"Human"...

11

HIDDEN KEYS

These little eyes
Don't remember quite clear
The innocent face
It once stared at in the mirror
-
These little hands
Once without blame
These lips part
To scream out my name
I LIE TO MYSELF
I AM
I AM
I AM.... FREE
I have hidden the keys
Back where memories park
Cannot retrieve
Afraid of the dark
So here I sit
On the curb of imagination
In the pit of emotional
Strangulation
I AM NOT... I LIE... I AM...
FREE

12

IT'S JUST A BIG ASK

♦

It's just a big ask
Utterly abandoning myself to God as I understand Him
What does that even mean?

As I understand Him?
What if it's a her?
Or simply non-binary, sexless.

Where has "He" been when I was alone?
How do you let a human endure such pain?
Maybe there should be a limit to free will
When it's used to harm others.

And I'm supposed to find "purpose in my pain"
Were they looking to find purpose in my pain as well?
Where were you God?

Were you with me?
And were you also with them?
How can you be both?

As I understand you - hmm...
You didn't seem to even care
How can I abandon myself to the care of that?
I see no hope of ever trusting you completely
So miracle it must be
Or you've lost before we've even began

But you have your ways
And I will never understand them
But that's where it gets interesting

Oh you are crafty, I'll give you that
Sending me others who feel it too
Having me connect others who are like me, with you

The problem is that I believe you love THEM
But have trouble seeing where I fit in
With the story I have received and lived

And oh you are crafty, I'll give you that
Making me care about their lives so much
Making me want to help them heal

And oh, you are so crafty
Distracting me while you heal my soul
Helping me unconsciously let the past go

It was such a big ask
And now I can no longer embrace how I felt
When the process all began...

When you were secretly holding my hand.
And preparing me for what you had planned.

13

A SONG FOR THE DEVIL

You're out of excuses
I'm out of time
Just keep your 2 cents baby
cause you ain't worth a dime

You twist the truth with style
without an ounce of shame
I'll still be right here baby
cause you'll need someone to blame
Step Right Up, I'll sell my soul for you
You and only you!

I am not your token
I am not your prize
I will not be broken
I will not play nice

My head on your shoulder
is like a chopping block
one moment I'm safe to sleep
The next you're cuttin' me off

You call it crazy baby
I call it lies
Are you a wolf? Or sheep?
It's such a good disguise!

Step Right Up, I'll sell my soul for you!
You and only you!

I am not your token
I am not your prize
I will not be broken
I will not play nice
(I! LOOOVE!!! YOOU!!!)

There's a little maze
In your little mind
Things you need to chase
Things you need to find
Tell a little tale
Tell a little lie
Kiss a little kiss
Rhyme a little rhyme
Can you hold your breath?
Maybe hold your tongue?
Can you tell me why?
Out from underneath your thumb...

Make sure it all rhymes
Cover your little eyes (little lies)

I am not your token
I am not your prize
I will not be broken
I will not play nice
(I! LOOOVE!!! YOOU!!!)

14

IGNORANCE

♦

The things I know about are these things.
And I may not know about those other things.
But I bet you'll tell me everything you know about
both of those things.

And then someone else who thinks they know more
things than you know about those things -
Will interject something about that thing -
Which will cause someone else to scream the
opposite thing
About the things you know some things about.

Then these new things can be argued about for days-
While other things come to light -
So that more people can contradict the things they
know nothing about -
With things they read or heard -
That were said by people who think they know things
about more things.

Even though they've never actually researched
anything - But they saw something by someone who says
they know more things -

About a thing someone else said about a thing they
know nothing about -

So they talk about the thing they heard someone else
talk about -

So they can seem like they know something too.

I don't even have to explain a thing about what this
poem is about... you know... you know.

And some of you -
Even though you know nothing about this thing-
You will definitely say some things about this thing -
So you won't look like you know nothing - about these
things.

Ain't that something?

15

A SONG FOR YOU

♦

If by chance - One day
You wake and find - That I am no longer by your side
I want you to go on without fear
Cause we did our best while I was here
Remember my heart is always near
If you... play this song again.

All my life - A suffocated light
We'll shine with all our might
You can't put me out - Don't put me out

Stand and fight - Next to me tonight
We'll shine with all our might
You can't put me out - Don't put me out

Deep in our hearts - A light shines bright
<u>But most people live in black & white</u>
Some will see it and turn it down
Others will try hard to put it out
Hear my voice as I scream and shout
LET IT SHINE!!!

All my life
A suffocated light
We'll shine with all our might
You can't put me out
Don't put me out

Stand and fight
Next to me tonight
We'll shine with all our might
You can't put me out
Don't put me out

Don't put your eyes down
Keep your chin up.... Smile
This prism is not your prison
You're not alone tonight
So get back up and fight
Stand on your own
And own what you've become
Become what you have known

All my life - A suffocated light
We'll shine with all our might
You can't put me out - Don't put me out

Stand and fight - Next to me tonight
We'll shine with all our might
You can't put me out - Don't put me out

16

NOT EVEN CLOSE!

I've got my mind made up
Cause baby I've had enough and
you don't know what that's like
He had a plan as well
We locked eyes as he left me for hell and
you don't know what that's like

That was so long ago
Knowing now what I know
Like everyone else
Who put me through hell
You're just too late
A dollar short
Not even close...

Don't say you know how I feel
In your attempt to help me to heal
Cause you don't know what that's like
When I shut off the lights
He haunts me in dreams at night
And you don't know what that's like

But that was so long ago
Knowing now what I know
Like everyone else
Who put me through hell
You're just too late
A dollar short
Not even close...

I close my eyes
I can't even say this part
Like it was even me
Feels like a dream
A nightmare ago...
I don't even know
How I feel anymore
My heart is SO SORE
That BULLET TORE!
Into the middle of my soul

Freedom past the wall
The song that says it all
I watched your body fall
Bloodstains on the wall
Aftermath of love
Hatred up above
The shit you did to me
The way I "used to be"

17

HAD TOO MUCH TO THINK TODAY

🌢

It's amazing
How many things that I do wrong
Inside my own mind
On any given day

And it's amazing
How when we're dancing on the clouds
How it all comes crashing down

Please forgive me
If I'm standing in your way
What can I say
I've had too much to think today

I know down deep I wasn't right for you
Although inside so bad I wanted to
Make you smile
But all the while
Chasing my dreams
I somehow lost you

Please forgive me if
I'm standing in your way
I never meant to hurt you

And I need you to hear me say

You were the sun in my skies
The light in my eyes
The songs I could not sing
And I...
Shhh...
Too much to think today

18

LITTLE JENNY

Little Jenny ain't got no self esteem
Little Jenny don't keep herself too clean
Little Jenny don't care who's around
Little Jenny's keeping herself down
But she says...

I don't mind - I don't mind
I don't mind... cause I - I'm so blind

She kneels down in the parking lot
She gave him everything that she's got
And she said... I'd rather die than be with you
With one more blow her life was through
But she said...

I don't mind - I don't mind
I don't mind... Cause I - I'll be fine

I don't mind - I don't mind
AS LONG AS IT'S NOT ME
THEN I... I'LL STAY BLIND!

19

THERE YA GO, KID

Past the ego...
through the judgments...
after the "I know that I know this"...
through the eyes of observation...
and under the radar of self-preservation ...
I have found a smile and a nod from God
and the message of "there ya go, kid..."
and it makes me happy..

X

20

QUARANTINE

And she heard in her mind that day...

"Mother Earth is very happy right now

As She continuously experiences lowered chemicals,
lowered attacks of her surface
and an earth wide shift of selfishness to love...

Maybe it was a foul idea to Her inhabitants to be
locked away in their homes -

But the fresh air outside was a sign of a healing earth
creating healthier air...
and a doorway to new mindfulness for those who
share her gifts.

The shift was happening and their eyes were beginning
to see..."

SO.. IT... IS

Who am I?
Am I a child of God?
Am I a loving human?
Am I a spiritual person?
Am I a friend to those who need one?
Am I a supportive person?
Am I part of the problem?
Am I part of the solution?

I am whoever I choose to be - at any moment -
of any day...
I do not need permission....
I do not need the right...
I am who and what I decide to be NOW.
And so it is....
And so are you...

MORPHINE LOLLIPOP

♦

I wish I had something
To quiet my head
Become a void instead
A Candy necklace made of valium
Or a morphine lollipop
Just to make the voices stop
Because-
All I hear is

La-Da - Da - Da - Da
It's in my head it's taking over
La-Da - Da - Da - Da
In my mind...

I try to shut you out
But your name
It won't leave my mouth
Your kiss still stains my lips
In my dreams I am hostage
To your fingertips
Because-
All I hear is

La-Da - Da - Da - Da
It's in my head it's takin over
La-Da - Da - Da - Da
It's in my mind
La-Da - Da - Da - Da
I need a morphine lollipop
La-Da - Da - Da - Da

Seems love was destined to find us
With a trail of scorched earth behind us
Your smile, is like a thousand cherry bombs
Exploding in my heart
It's been there from the start

Your eyes that cut me straight to the core
The heart that's falling down and begging for more
The chains that tighten down and lock to the floor
If you want me I'm yours

La-Da - Da - Da - Da
It's in my head it's takin over
La-Da - Da - Da - Da
It's in my mind
La-Da - Da - Da - Da
It's in my head it's takin over...
La-Da - Da - Da - Da
God Damnit baby...

DIRTY GIRL

Dirty Girl
Seek & Destroy
Dirty Girl
Every asshole's toy
Walk into the room...
My radar starts to boom

Psycho Chick
I've been that once or twice
Psycho Chick
I'm evil then I'm nice
Pick me up just once...
Regret it for the rest of your life

Dirty Girl ... Dirty Girl... ha ha ha
Dirty Girl, I'm a Dirty Girl, Ha ha ha ha ha
Dirty Girl ... Dirty Girl... ha ha ha
Dirty Girl, I'm a Dirty Girl, Ha ha ha ha ha!

Dirty Girl
I'll please you, then I'm gone
Dirty Girl
Take me home to mom
Let her see the one

Who'll twist you til' you're spun
Psycho Chick
I think you're being used
Psycho Chick
I think you like abuse
Think you've got the upper hand?
You'll never understand

I'm A Dirty Girl ... Dirty Girl... ha ha ha
Dirty Girl, I'm a Dirty Girl, Ha ha ha ha ha
Dirty Girl ... Dirty Girl... ha ha ha
Dirty Girl, I'm a Dirty Girl, Ha ha ha ha ha!

Ha ha ha ha ha ha ha ha haaaaa!

24

THINK!

Obsession
Compulsion
Attraction
Rejection
Affection
Affliction
Anger
Resentment
Revenge
Discontent
Remorse
Pity... DRINK!

Lies
Manipulation
Retaliation
Guilt
Degradation
Fake love
Demoralization
Insecurity
Grandiosity
Smother me!
Leave me... DRINK!

Broke
Jobless
Homeless
Friendless
Careless
Angry
Don't like me?
Then leave me!
Believe me...
You're not me

.45
.25
.357
Shotgun
Knife
Rope
Gas
Chickenshit
Dumbass...
DRINK!

JUST STAY

●

I ... just... can't... go on
I... can't... get... numb enough
I... can't ... quiet... my head
I... wish...

Look in the mirror
I recognize those eyes
One more drink and
She will fade away

Almost there
One more shot and I won't care
One more time
She is fine...

But she won't go away!
She won't stay away!
She'll be back tomorrow!
Why won't she go away?!

Every time I see her
I'm filled with rage
Everyone likes her
But they don't know
what's in my head

I close my eyes
One more time...
I close my eyes...
Ahhhhh

She won't go away
She won't go away
She'll be back tomorrow
Why won't she go away!

You think that it's over - now that you're sober???

I just can't go on
I can't get numb enough
I can't quiet my head
I wish... I wish I was dead!

I won't go away
I won't fade away
I'll be back tomorrow
Why won't I go away?

You think that it's over - Now that you're sober

Your freedom won't come - from a bottle - or a gun

I - Will - Never - Go - Away!

26

SCREAM

You make me want to SCREAM!
You may think I'm
Bitter
Or jaded
Or out of touch
Someday's I'm your little angel and I...
I mean so much
Somedays I look at you and I
I start to dream
But other days I look at you
AND I JUST WANT TO SCREAM!

Feel the passion
Feel the drive
One more reason to stay alive
Feed the anger
Feed the need
One more reason you make me want to
Feel the passion
Feel the drive
One more reason to stay alive
Feed the anger
Feed the need
One more reason to make me bleed.

I see your big "personality"
And I know what you're good for
I hear your words
I listen to your fucking
"Passion" ... ugh
But in the end
I remember who you really are (oh yeah)
You tell me that you love me?!
And I just want to SCREAM!

Feel the passion
Feel the drive
One more reason to stay alive
Feed the anger
Feed the need
One more reason you make me want to
Feel the passion
Feel the drive
One more reason to stay alive
Feed the anger
Feed the need
One more reason to make me bleed.

27

HERE WE GROW AGAIN

I looked in the mirror today and saw a different person behind my eyes staring back at me....

She was less cautious and more grateful and wise... although her experiences were mine, the feelings were ones I didn't recognize...

Love, where there was once only hatred, had replaced the darkness with light...

The chains, had fallen from my arms and were in piles on the floor...

Here we grow again.

28

AN UNINSPIRED QUOTE

"... when feeling uninspired
it could be wise to spend your time
looking for others to inspire you...

...

but it is even wiser to take some quiet
time to uncover the inspiration within
yourself..."

X

29

I DID IT AGAIN

So I'm lying in my bed
And I open my eyes
I look to the right
And I don't recognize the person next to me

And my head is pounding
And the room is spinning and...
Oh my god...
What did I do the night before?

I can't find my car
And I haven't been home for days and...
Oh my god...
I slept with a midget.

It doesn't matter, it's always the same thing
I say to myself:
"Franki, you did it again."
And again, and again and again and again and ahhhh!

Not gonna fuck him again, he's a stupid prick!
Not smoking drugs no more, not even for kicks!
I'm gonna sober up cause God I feel like shit
I'm gonna sober up,

JUST ONE MORE TIME and then that's it!

I did it again, did it again, did it again... ahhhh.

Not doing speed no more,
I've had 2 heart attacks
Not sleeping around no more
I'm tired of being on my back!
I'm gonna sober up
I'm gonna quit that crap...
I'm gonna sober up... JUST ONE MORE TIME AND THEN THAT'S THAT!

I did it again, I did it again, did it again, did it again...

You ever said this prayer?
God, if you get me out of this one...
I swear, I'll never drink again
I'll sober up
I'll go to church
Come on God...
Let's make a deal!
One more time...
Get me out of this one...
Come on God!

Ah - fuck it.

I did it again!

30

THE BEAUTY THAT IS LOVE

I used to think I knew what love looked like,
I used to think I knew what it felt to be loved...
But I was mistaken.
Until the day God temporarily took my eyesight.

If only for a little time.
I was forced to see the world through foggy lenses,
Shadows where there used to be details of faces,
flowers and words.

I was struggling to make out the color of her eyes,
The big - beautiful eyes that stared through to my soul
since the day she was born. And then it was dull... her
eye color. I missed it.

I was clumsy, unstable with my body... then the mind
followed. The more I tried to be self-sufficient, the
worse it got.
Scared to ask for help. Scared to admit I was scared.
Scared to face the fact that I couldn't help myself out
of this one. I give love... I don't ask for love - my mind
reminded me.   And then the voice of something
bigger shouted it out to a room full of people. I cried,
uncontrollably and I told them...

I cannot see anymore... everything is foggy - I'm afraid - I feel helpless - I feel weak.
Wait... "felt"... I "felt" weak...
Yet, I had no idea that would be one of the strongest things I would ever do.
Humbly, without reservation or control. I asked for help.

Love is so much bigger and so much more powerful than I ever could've imagined.
I soon became grateful to something wiser than me - for taking my eyesight.
Because it was in the lack of sight that I became able to see more clearly what is truly important.

The giving & receiving of unconditional LOVE... the connectedness to other humans.
Allowing others to support me when I am broken or afraid.

I couldn't see anything well enough outside - and so I had to look within. There it was that I found the light... in the darkness.

And now I know what love truly looks like...
It is always double sided - never one sided. Love is receiving, not just giving.

Love is the light... in the darkness... and it needs no vision to see it at all... so look with your heart - close your eyes and ignore all that is "visual." There you will truly see THE BEAUTY THAT IS LOVE. ✗

31

HUMANITY IS DESTROYING HUMANITY

Humanity is destroying humanity.
Negativity Is a breeding ground for more negativity...
Hatred swells and gives birth to more hatred.
Confusion feeds them all.

Double entendres
Crafted as the manipulators best friend
For even saying exactly what they mean
You do not understand

They take, take, take
Selling assurance of survival
The fittest and best
Bred to compete now as rivals

Robbing us of our freedom
While selling us all security
And we sign up with smiles
No, you don't understand me.

Humans killing humans
Nothing physical - just in our head
With hierarchy bred in chambers
Our dreams, our passion - dead

If the masses look around now
At what's left of the human race
Where once there was wonder and dreams
Lay shells of bodies - with empty faces

But there is a spark afoot
For Universe won't stand by
And allow all this beauty to shrivel
Or the vibrational consciousness die

For just the same as it was unraveled
By the same means it will rebuild
The vortex has opened among us
And knowledge around us is spilled

Humanity is destroying Humanity
But Humanity is also rebuilding as well
For the humanity that has been bred
Will be the humanity that soon will have fell

32

THE MERCHANT KNOWN AS EGO

♦

I
Simple child
Grown adult
Holding on to buyers remorse
The purchase?
Guilt, shame, self hatred and fear.
Signing up again and again to meet with the ego
The ego, selling me useless opinions, thoughts and ideas
It shows up quiet and still...
Egging me on... and taunting me
Like a fucking car salesman
Seemingly wanting to help me out
But in the end - I am left with something which has no real purpose and serves me nothing in return
But I am growing
I am learning
I am rising up and settling down - all at the same time
To a place in the middle... a place of calm balance

The merchant known as ego
Complicated and controlling
Crafty & persuasive
Looking to find a weakness to exploit it
Peddling pieces of fear into my very core
It has an agenda. But it is confused

It thinks it's trying to keep me safe
Safe from those who may hurt me or exploit me
But really it ends up keeping me isolated
From everyone who may have been able to get close
Instead, placing me above or below those around me.

And we fight now
I fucking body slam that shit into the concrete!
Because FUCK GUILT - fuck self-sabotage - fuck fear -
fuck the stories I was taught as a child.

I wasn't born with guilt
I was given it
I wasn't born with shame
I was sold it
I wasn't born with fear
I inherited it
All the negative feelings added to me after the fact
They are not mine - they were never meant to be a
part of me
So why do I keep buying it again?

This merchant known as ego...
I am done being a patron
Done buying into that which separates me from those
around me
Instead, I open my arms and embrace it all...
Even the merchant known as ego
I embrace... but am no longer a customer

33

AH, THE BEAUTIFUL PAIN

♦

Ah, the beautiful pain
Do I hurt?
Yes, I hurt too.
And what shall I do with this pain?
Hide it?
Shame it?
Nurture it?
No, I shall do neither of these.
I shall honor it
I shall love it
I shall give it the acknowledgment it deserves
It is mine
Mine alone
And mine to share, if I so choose

Even the pain I received from my own choices
The burdens and the darkness
It has served me well
It has taught me
It has strengthened me
It has given me vision for hope
I shall respect the pain and its' process

For it will bring me clarity

From clarity, I shall find understanding
Through understanding, insight
From insight, experience
From experience, introspection
From introspection, I shall make a way
Shine a light for all who come after me
A new vision for the future
Stories of the past
Knowledge and wisdom to pass on
And this... this shall create hope

From hope will spring love,
From love, passion
From passion, forgiveness
From forgiveness, nurturing
From nurturing... compassion
From compassion, a new future

Ah, my friend...
The beautiful pain.

Let it not be wasted on me.

34

WORDSMITH

What if every WORD you uttered out loud, or put in to the "air"was responsible for creating your future experiences...

You say WORDS of hate and judgment - and you inspire those around you to do the same... utter your WORDS.

You want them to jump on your bandwagon- give you a "thumbs up" for your negativity...

And if you're lucky - your WORDS are repeated and shared so that others can create more of the same with those who will listen to them - and agree - and repeat.

Next thing you know... well - you can see where this is going.

Now imagine the opposite...

What if every WORD you uttered out loud, or put in to the "air"was responsible for creating your future experiences...

You say WORDS of love and forgiveness - and you inspire those around you to do the same... utter your WORDS.

You want them to jump on your bandwagon- give you a "thumbs up" for your positivity...

And if you're lucky - your WORDS are repeated and shared so that others can create more of the same with those who will listen to them - and agree - and repeat.

Next thing you know... well - you can see where this is going.

35

ASSHOLE

I say I love you and you laugh at me...
Cause you're just an asshole like the rest

Asshole... asshole
Why won't you talk to me?
Why won't you look at me?
You said you cared for me!
You said you loved me!
You're an asshole... an asshole.

I try to leave
But then you're sweet to me
And then next week
You just won't speak to me
Asshole... asshole

When I get mad
Then you get nice
A psycho cycle
I pay the price
Cause you're an asshole... an asshole

Someday it's gonna end

Someday you'll pay, my friend
Someday I'll turn and run
Someday I'm killed for fun
Asshole... ashhole

I won't wine - you won't give me pity
I don't whine - you don't give me pity
You're an asshole... an asshole

I'm weak - you say
Why don't I go away?
But then next week
You're begging me to stay
Asshole... asshole

You say you love me and I laugh at you...
Cause now I'm just an asshole like the rest

36

THE WAYWARD GRIFFIN

You are the Griffin
You are supposed to be noble
You are meant to be protective
But you have lost your way
I used to look upon you
With such wonder and respect
How you would fight to the death
Stomping out evil and corruption
You were so beautiful to me
But now your talons are broken
Your wings have been clipped
Your heart has been darkened
Your morals have slipped
But you're not without hope
You're not doomed to continue
But you must make this choice
To return to The Source
Or continue your training
With your painful discourse
But I believe in you oh Griffin
Who you were meant to be
A protector of man
A protector of me

37

THE MIRROR

I write things on the mirror to remind myself what I always forget. To be nice to me. You see, I can be nice to anyone else, even in the middle of them attacking me. It's a gift. A curse. Sad. I'm not sure if it's me being weak or strong. If you ask 10 different people, the opinions vary. Either way, chances are, if you don't like me, I'll most likely be nice to you.

I used to joke that I could walk into a room, and there could be 100 people in this room. If 99 people liked me and 1 didn't, I could only focus on that one person. For some reason, I had to know what their problem was. Add a little bit of alcohol and whatever perceived problem I imagine they had with me would quickly become a reality. Like it or not. We were gonna "handle the situation".

I digress though. As I was saying earlier, I remind myself to be kind to me on my bathroom mirror. I write things like. "Love yourself" and "You are exactly where you are supposed to be at this moment".

38

TORE UP

♦

I see you out - in all the younger bars
You like little boys - the ones that play guitars
You shove your fat - in little leather pants
And your gut hangs out and it jiggles while you dance

Because you're tore up - tore up from the floor up
That's right I said you're tore up - tore up from the floor
up

In 73' you were the young hot thing
You were the beauty in every kind of scene
In 83' you hit the big 4-0
You're tore up grandma - and you don't even know

Because you're tore up - tore up from the floor up

That's right I said you're tore up - tore up from the floor
up

The time has come to put away your heals
When holding on to youth - you've stole all you could
steal
They take you home and kill all of your fears
But you only look good after drinking 20 beers

Because you're tore up - tore up from the floor up

That's right I said you're tore up - tore up from the floor up

And in case you haven't gotten it yet grandma
Let me tell you one more time

Because you're tore up - tore up from the floor up
That's right I said you're tore up - tore up from the floor up

39

THEY ARE WAITING

●

They are waiting for you to fail
They are waiting for you to drink
They are waiting for you to say it out loud
But they care not what you really think

They are setting you up for failure
They are betting on your demise
They are sending you messages of confusion
They are selling you buckets of lies

They are laughing at every emotion
Milking tears from your innocent heart
They are colluding behind your back
Buying stock in you falling apart

They wake up 20 minutes before you
As you wake from a nighttime of rest
They start screaming their bitter opinions
They're intended to keep you depressed

They are only inside your mind
Delusional versions of you
But you pray, and recover now daily
Cause you realize that none of it's true

40

CRITICISM

🌢

"Honesty
Without LOVE
Is Brutality"

✗

41

AN HONORABLE NON-DEATH

💧

She.
One minute old.
And they took her away.
I lay there confused. But couldn't think clearly.
The red was around me.
On the floor... somethings wrong.
The voices, they faded into mumbles.
The bed - it moved with a jerk.
The lights, they flew past my field of vision.
The doctor, he grabbed my face.
You are dying... do you understand me?
I did.
I begged God... please let me live.
But I realized, it was my time to go. So I prayed...
Please let my children know that I loved them...
And let them know you.
And I let go. Without fear... feeling totally loved.

Days later... It felt like flying through the air
And smacking with a powerful thud back into my body
The pain... everywhere... **I am not dead.** I wouldn't
hurt this bad if I was dead.
I am trapped... in the body.
My eyes won't open. My chest won't work
I cannot speak. And my hands are tied to the bed.

I am not dead.

I can hear them talking around me
I can hear them crying
They are letting me go...
And in the middle of the night, I think
An angel spoke into my ear
"You have to choose to live"
"You have to choose to breathe"

Days later, my eyes open, but I cannot speak with this tube
So I wiggle my hand... "get her a pen"
And I write one word - it was hard to breathe
BABY... They tell me "She is fine"
And they brought me a polaroid
There she was
The most beautiful new soul on earth
And I knew in that instant
That I had to live.

I felt guilt for surviving... because I thought I wasn't worthy
I felt I was a terrible mother, and they were doomed with me
I narrowly escaped an honorable death
But I did not choose to die... I chose to live
And you are reading this now because I found purpose
I found the truth about my worth and why I was saved
She. One week old and her sister and brother at home.

She was my purpose.

42

TELL ME DO YOU HATE ME

I've seen more
Than little eyes should see
Six years old
And a tragedy
I pray to God won't you set me free?
Why do you let him put his hands on me?

Tell me do you hate me?
Tell me have I done something wrong?
Tell me as he takes me...
Tell me why you let this go on?
Tell me why...
Tell me why...
And tell me can you hear me?
Oh where have you gone?

All alone with no place to hide
I tell my mother but she pushes me aside
Sent me away to ease her shame
So tell me why am I the one she blames?

Tell me do you hate me?
Tell me have I done something wrong?

Tell me as she leaves me...
Tell me why you let this go on?
Tell me why...
Tell me why...
And tell me can you hear me?
Oh where have you gone?

And now that I have grown
I sing this song
The years revealed to me
Who was right and wrong
You were always there
Lightning up my way
I could not see it then
But it's so clear today

Tell me that you love me
And tell me that I've done nothing wrong
Tell me as you take me
Tell me why you let this go on
Tell me why
Tell me why
Cause I know you can heal me

43

BECAUSE OF YOU

🌢

I'm trapped inside this house
Tortured by secrets
Oh what could be more confusing
To a girl like me, than this?

I see your face in every corner of my room
When I wake, when I sleep
Everywhere I look it's you
But now I realize...

My heart is stronger because of you
I sing this song here because of you
I've learned to live on because of you
Because of you... I made it through.

I want to taste revenge
Beg for forgiveness
Oh what could be more confusing
To a boy like you, than this?

It's been so many years
Angers come and gone
But thanks to you
I've had the strength to carry on
And now I realize...

My heart is stronger because of you
I sing this song here because of you
I've learned to live on because of you

Because of you... I made it through.

44

STEP RIGHT UP

♦

I see the Ferris wheel
Go up and down
Plastic Horses they make no sound
But the merry-go-round is flying
Out of control
And the bearded lady has stolen my soul

I try to jump but it won't slow down
I know that soon is another town
Of people standing in line
To distract them from their own lives
Lonely children - husbands - and wives

I'm standing in a bad dream
I'm wishing I could just wake up right now
He's finding where I hide and scream
It's a never ending, ending all around
Down a hallway through a big door
Through a chamber that's alive to lock me out
How is it that the walls see
Decisions I have made before I'm out?

I am standing on a
Carnival ride - you can

Meet me outside
We could leave our cares behind
And if your family shows, I'll pretend I am blind

It makes no difference,
I'm YOUR NEW BEST FRIEND
I'm the beginning and the end
A distraction around every bend
I am everything you've ever wanted - and more

I'm standing in a bad dream
I'm wishing I could just wake up right now
He's finding where I hide and scream
It's a never ending - ending all around
Down a hallway through a big door
Through a chamber that's alive to lock me out
How is it that the walls see
Decisions I have made before I'm out?

You can't leave me!
Someday you'll love me...
I'm so easy
Cause I'm on your side...

45

THINGS I SHOULD'VE SAID

♦

I'm not blind
I owe you an apology
But how do I tell you I was wrong?

It seems you're doing fine
Maybe better off without me
So I'll just put it in this song

I love your laugh
Your eyes
The way that you smile
Every morning in your bed

And when you kiss my face
The music, I heard
Playing in my head...

Things I should've said

The Grey Goose and the wine
Not a moment there was unkind
Though the psycho ex boyfriend wasn't fun

I know I ran away

Here's the thing... I couldn't say
I was afraid you could've been the one

I love your laugh
Your eyes
The way that you smile
Every morning in your bed

And when you kiss my face
The music, I heard
Playing in my head...

Things I should've said

46

MAYBE IT'S NOT ME

Yes it hurts,
And it's embarrassing to admit right now
I'd say I'm wrong
But shame on me, I just don't know how

I could grow to be better
I could just stay the same
Don't really matter
We both know
It's me you need to blame

I've got this problem
With shutting down when the timings wrong
We could talk
But it's a waste of words that have no song

You'll like this note
Cause it grips you with all of its' might
It goes - oooooooh - inside

Yes I'm weak
And yes I'd speak
If the words would just come out
But the words they won't come out

If I'm the problem here
Then why am I in tears?
Maybe it's not me... maybe it's not me.

I can't stay
While you sit and hide in this misery
You call me unloyalw
But watching you choose this is killing me
So I'll write this note
When you wake up it's all you will find
Cause - oooooooh - I tried

Yes I'm weak
Yes, I'd speak
If the words would just come out
But the words they won't come out

If I'm the problem here
Then why am I in tears
Maybe it's not me... maybe it's not me.

47

BROKEN ME

Don't go away,
I'm your puppet on a string
Don't throw away -
Broken me

Everyone is asking me if I love you
Well I hate you cause
You threw away broken me

And you're not satisfied
With my heart
No baby now you want my soul!

Everybody's asking me if I love you
Well I hate you case
You threw away broken me

Don't go away
I'm your puppet on a string
Don't throw away
Broken me

Tell me now
Is this the game

The game we play with you and me?
All the while you're breaking me

And you're not satisfied
With my heart
No baby now you want my soul!

Everybody's asking me if I love you
Well I hate you case
You threw away broken me

48

TRAINWRECK TINA

(In memory of Lance Romance)

Trainwreck Tina was a ballroom ballerina
Owns a rock show up in the sky
Lance Romance wasn't scared to take a chance
When she showed up and said "Hop inside!"

Boy I'm not lying, 20 seconds after dying
Tina may show up for you
Well there's thunder and lightning
From the earth it looks frightening
But upstairs there's a whole different view!

There's a stage in the sky
Where there's a show every night!
If Trainwreck Tina shows up there when you die
Well, she will take you for the ride... of your life
To Trainwreck Tinas

All the musicians who were vying for positions
On the earth down here while alive
Blow the doors down with a deafening sound
At Trainwreck Tinas each night

From ceiling to floor and going straight out the door
Is a list that she hangs up with pride
There's a line into Heaven and a line into hell

But if you're lucky you just might get inside

Cause, there's a stage in the sky
Where there's a show every night!
If Trainwreck Tina shows up there when you die
Well, she will take you for the ride... of your life
To Trainwreck Tinas

Operator: *Trainwreck Tinas, how can I help you?*
Woman: Uh, I think I must have dialed wrong,
Operator: *How can I help you?*
Woman: I was trying to call 911. I've been in a car accident, there's people all over the place
Operator: *Ma'am, I need you to listen, just calm down... Trainwreck Tina's on her way*
Woman: What do you mean Trainwreck Tina's on her way?
Operator: *You've got a show in 2 hours*
Woman: What are you talking about, I've got a show in 2 hours?!
Operator: *We'll see you soon*
Woman: Listen, you're not listening to me, I'm trying to get through to you... I may be dying over here!
Operator: *I hate to be the one to tell you this, but you're already dead.*
Woman: Nooooo!

There's a stage in the sky
Where there's a show every night!
If Trainwreck Tina shows up there when you die
Well, she will take you for the ride... of your life

To Trainwreck Tinas.

49

FLY ON THE WALL

◆

He's slapping her face
She's put in her place
It's love in the sickest way
But she always stays

She's saying it's done
But he isn't gone
Comes bursting through the door
And he's got a gun

And I'm a fly
And I saw
Everything that night
The tears she cries.........

Her heart is in pain
She's over this game
She's not playing this time
The trigger's pulled

He's watching her scream
She's watching him fall
Sulfur it burns her nose
And his eyes go cold

And I'm a fly
And I saw
Everything that night
The tears she cries... they never end.
In my head, words you said
"Franki, I love you, here watch this!"
Ahhh!

My heart, my mind
Died with him that night
And I don't know
What to put next

I'm a fly
And I saw everything that night
And I'm a fly
And I saw everything that night

The tears she cries...
They never... they never ... they never end!

50

THE FAT FUCK & THE WHORE

(In memory of Gabby Gaborno)

I know they won't understand this
Because it's between you and me
Matching tattoos
Decades of laughter. And standing on a stage
Singing for thousands of people together
It started with the day you lost God
And you called me to tell me He's gone
In prison... you... and a collect call
17 years hanging over your head
I was the only one you said you trusted to tell this to
We spoke for hours... you never paid for my phone bill
But I told you to let God reveal himself to you
Stop looking, you haven't lost him, you are merely afraid
C'mon you fat fuck... You got this
And then a miracle, and a judge... heard a voice, set you free.
He set you free...
To hold my hand next
To bring me into my element
But I was insecure
And I'm afraid
So you walk up and put your arms around me

C'mon ya little whore... You got this
But what if I bomb?
You got this
A whore sells herself to anyone who buys
And they're all buying kiddo. Just breathe
As he turns around and gives me a wink
And he walks out to the microphone
I stood there... my breath escaped my lungs
I need air to sing... too many people... I'm frozen
You saw... and you walked over and whispered in my ear
You're a whore
To which I whispered back... and you're a fat fuck
And we sang... and sang... and sang for years.

On the week before you died
I tried so hard to get through
But you were too weak to speak
The cancer had won
But I remembered our last conversation
When we spoke of your sickness and imminent death
You told me you knew God was there
And had no doubts... and you thanked me for bringing you back to God.
And I said you should never have trusted a whore
To which you replied
What do I know? I'm just a fat fuck.

I miss you. My friend. My rock. My brother. My fat fuck.

51

NEWEST GUARDIAN ANGEL

(In memory of Emily Rose)

Another life together
I think we did just fine
Laying in your bed beside you
Watching you sleep
Feeling such helplessness
Knowing this is your end
Snatching up every conversation I can get
Crying in silence, knowing you can't see me anymore
I ask myself as I watch you breathe
Would I go back and trade it all in?
Would I choose to avoid this pain by never meeting you?
No. No. No. No. No.
I would choose the pain.
I would choose the struggle.
I would choose to do it all over again.
Because you are my angel, and I am yours.
I used to think I was here to save you
But I see now that it's the exact opposite.
You are here to save me.
I am a runner
I run when I get close
But you have told me I'm not allowed to run anymore
You're the one who is dying

And I'm not allowed to run away to avoid the pain this time
And you're not doing this without me
So suck it up... and deal with it.
But fuck this hurts
I can't help you
I can't give you anything to help you out of this
And you're blind... the pressure has taken your sight
So if God is in everything that happens, why did you go blind?
I asked you one night.
To which you replied... it took me going blind to be able to see what's truly important.
You have no need for money, make-up or things
You need only LOVE...
Nothing else matters, but love.
You will leave me soon - I know this.
I'm not prepared
But I am all-in
I would sign up for this again
I would do it a million times
To have the memories I will keep when you leave
To have the tears and the laughter we shared
I would choose the pain of this over and over again
I fear tonight will be the last time I see you
But I don't feel robbed even one little bit
I am the richest Godmother on earth
Because I am your earth angel
And soon, you will be my newest guardian angel

(Emily died the next day)

52

VEGANIGNORANCE

Vegan
Annoying - you call me
Overbearing - you label me
Plants have feelings too ya know - you sarcastically tell me
But have you ever heard a plant scream while being led to the slaughter?
I can't imagine being born, into a cage
Surviving in a cage
Herded, overfed, abused, tortured
Then killed... inhumanely
To be consumed
To be wasted
And I can't imaging not living, and being alive.
You don't have to be vegan to have my respect
But at least, be mindful about your consumption
Oh.. yeah... Fuck your annoying veganism...
Ok...
Fuck me... fuck my veganism
But first...
Fuck your ignorance
Fuck your arrogance
Fuck your inhumanity
Fuck your judgments
And fuck you too. ✗

53

ABOUT TO BE REPLACED

Looking into the future

She lies in another mans arms

He smiles - and listens

She responds to his charms

When she's crying, he's dying

You can see it on his face

It's the look of the man

Who's about to be replaced...

And this is why...

And this is why...

And this is why...

I continue to try.

54

THE TALL ONE

You may not know that this was written for you
Because I've taught you not to think this world revolves
around you
I've told you to rid the ego of it's powerful woo
But I am talking about you
I'm writing about you

The impressive soul you have become
The way you face your fears bravely
And admit your faults freely
The way you get angry about stupid things
And then call me to laugh it over
The way you have tried to push me away
With your loudness, and your angry words
Only to thank me for not abandoning you

The way you love that firefighter you have at home
The way you support him when he is gone
The way you've become so gentle
The way you nurture those around you
And show up in the middle of the night to save a life
The way you rescue so many animals
Although I think you may have a problem there

My tall tall friend, I adore you
And I know that we could truly never see eye to eye
But only because you're too tall and my eyes don't reach that high

But with our hearts, we see perfectly
One mind healing the other
You're my teacher
My equal
A soul contract discovered

I am impressed by your passion
Your talents
Your glory
Your strength
Your honestly
Your lack of "poor me"

I want you to know that you've taught me so much
Thank you for asking me to be your support
Thank you for being mine
My friend, my mirror
The South to my North

55

THE BEST OF BOTH WOLVES

♦

The best of both wolves
Let me ponder this for a moment
One wolf is anger, regret, self-pity, greed
The other is love, humility, kindness, truth
These all live inside us
I have them inside me
I see them inside you
My sweet daughter
My little wolf
My Mowgli
You have taught me strength
You have overfilled me with Love
You have tested my heart
You have healed my heart as well
Your name... Bryanna... means strong woman
I chose it because of this
I was weak when I first met you
I felt little... insecure... not good enough for you
But you loved me
With everything your little heart had
You represented the fight between both wolves for me
Which one would I feed?
I watched you grow, and struggle, and thrive
I watched you choose life

And those little feet I used to wash in my hands
Walk the path of strength and determination now
And I'm not sure I had anything to do with that at all
But I am here
I will stand by your side, not matter what
Forever
I am so proud of you
I am so impressed with the woman you've chosen to be
I love you
You are...
The Best of Both Wolves

56

I THINK MY MIND IS MADE UP

I've got a secret
That maybe I shouldn't tell
I see his eyes, his lips, his smile
And I know I've already fallen

But I stare at you, in front of me
Your late nights
The bartenders named Darkness
And I lay awake
Sober... and not fooled
I have heard the messages
Seen the texts
And I know...
But you won't listen when I tell you to go
I don't love you
I barely even like you

You are arrogant
Mean
Selfish
Empty

The music you play is soulless
But the songs he sings are full

And I'm afraid I cannot hold it back
You simply need to go

And he has no idea, that I write him poems
And my lyrics are about a fantasy
That never will come true
But he has shown me
I don't love you

I try
But I don't love you
You are unlovable
Because you have no idea what Love even is

It's not late nights with other women
It's not using your money to keep me holding on
I've gone without money before
But love... having no love between us
That is a bankruptcy I can't afford

57

A WAY TO SLIP OUT

A thousand miles from home
Playing one more show
In a strange town
The loneliness has become numb
The only time I feel alive is on a stage
Singing... feeding off the energy of the crowd
And I like it loud, I like it loud

There's a band on the bill
And I'm sure they are good
But the crowd is quite packed
So I exit the room
And I hear it... I hear him
I feel his soul in his voice

I freeze... as his voice calls me
Back into the room
And in the middle of the crowd
I am seemingly illuminated
As he looks my way... and sings only to me

The room has become empty
The moment is frozen in time
He sings to me... Let Go - Live!

The voice is raspy and full
His pain connects with my soul
He is a wounded musician
With a wounded musicians heart
And we recognize each other with ease

I know him
For he is part of me
And I don't know the words
But I feel my heart sing
Don't hold me... too tightly
I might find a way to slip out.

And the years go by
And the marriage has run dry
I find myself alone for the first time in years
And as I call the number
I was given so long ago
He answers the phone and says
I've been waiting for your call.

58

EPICURUS, LEUCIPPUS & DEMOCRITUS

Across the ages you have spoken
Yet very few hear your words
An Atom...
Colliding with an Atom...
Colliding with Atoms...
Makes you.
Makes me.
Makes my desk.
Makes that tree.
Makes the ground.
Makes the candles.
Makes the animals.
Makes the sword.
Makes my friends.
Makes my so called enemies.

No differentiation at all
Between these Atoms
So what are we really?
Are we the desk?
Are we the sword?
Are we our so called enemies?
And so on and so forth

So if - at an atomic level
We cannot tell the Atom of a sword
From the Atom of our bodies
Then everything is alive.
Everything.

And Atoms
Creating energy
Holding energy
Emitting energy
Not one Atom being differentiated from another Atom
Suggests that everything thinks

Everything feels
Everything speaks
Everything is identical
Everything is you
Kind of makes me wonder
If I should pay more attention to the feelings of my
surroundings
Be more aware of the energy I bring to everything around
me
If they are me
And they are you
Then I am you
And you are me as well

A Perspective shift of this magnitude could change the
world

59

I'D LIKE YOU ALL TO KNOW

I'd like you all to know
I wear my scars proud
I sing of my successes
And failures out loud
I bare my soul
For you to critique
I lay out my pain
For the comfort you seek
Save Me -
Give Meaning To "ME"
Sing my words...
Set me free.
I've seen more
Than little eyes should see
But I seek nothing
Not sympathy
I just want to make sure
I give purpose to my shame
Not wasting a tear
Of inspired pain
Save Me -
Give Meaning To "ME"
Sing my words... Set me free. ✘

60

HIDDEN KEYS

These little eyes
Don't remember quite clear
The innocent face
It once stared at in the mirror
-
These little hands
Once without blame
These lips part
To scream out my name
I LIE TO MYSELF
I AM
I AM
I AM.... FREE
I have hidden the keys
Back where memories park
Cannot retrieve
Afraid of the dark
So here I sit
On the curb of imagination
In the pit of emotional
Stragulation
I AM NOT... I LIE... I AM...
FREE

61

NO FAIR!

♦

I got on my knees
I prayed
I begged
You stayed....

We were sick
Then I got well
Go to hell
You said.....

CHORUS
No Fair...!!
No Fair...!!
I swear!!!!!! I swear!!!
I'm Stuck in the middle of...Nowhere!

It's all good
You never could
Give me..
Now I see...

But Am I mad?
No- sad...
It's the best
I've never had

No Fair...!!
No Fair...!!
I swear!!!!!! I swear!!!
I'm Stuck in the middle of...Nowhere!

Why You? Why You?
WHY ME? WHY ME?
****

NO FAIR NO FAIR NO FAIR!!!!!!
No Fair...!!
No Fair...!!
I swear!!!!!! I swear!!!
I'm Stuck in the middle of...Nowhere!

62

ASSHOLES, POKIN' HOLES

So grateful to everyone I've ever encountered in my life

The good - not so good - you served a purpose

There is no such thing as regret when you are living a purpose filled life

Those assholes who poke holes in the bottom of your boat will teach you how to repair your own boat

They'll also teach you how to recognize an asshole before you let him on your boat

63

THE TRUTH SHALL SET YOU FREE

♦

THE TRUTH SHALL SET YOU FREE...
That's the simplified version of this statement.
We spend so much time pretending not to be the who
we are. We pretend not to be talented and powerful
because we are afraid of not living up to that always...
Or we are scared of what people will think...
And then some of us pretend not to be fucked up
because we don't want people to think bad about
us ...
Or we just don't like to look bad. It's freeing to be able
to own the good and the bad...

To tell everyone... hey, I'm fucked up sometimes!

Because that gives us a realistic starting point. I can't
fix something I don't acknowledge is broken.
Me... I got a LOT of good wrapped up with some self
defeating shit too...
The good thing is that I don't have to waste the energy
trying to convince you or I that the truth us something
different than what it is...
I can use ALL MY ENERGY effectively...

I'm busy working on fixin' shit today. You're welcome
to join.

64

BRING BACK THE TRUTH

I'm quite sure that there is no one on earth, who is always 100% impeccable with their word.

But I do know many who like myself strive to be.
Although I fall short of what my chosen ideal would be quite often.

When I find I've fallen short and have not been impeccable with my word, sometimes I find it necessary to reflect on what the truth is - own it - and even go as far as to <u>bringing truth where I have brought non truth.</u>

For example- when I have not been impeccable with my word- I feel it.

Maybe I think I haven't caused any damage to anyone because they are just words- but the person I've gossiped to or said bad things about another person to may now have an opinion- not of their own which I have poisoned them with.
The only way for me to fix that for myself is to bring the truth.

Which sometimes lies inside me- attached to some kind of fear.

When I bring the truth to that person it has the power to unlock their belief system and allow them to have a fresh experience and form their own opinions.

I am allergic to milk- I can tell someone that drinking milk will harm them- but what may be true for one person may not be the experience of another. (Imagine how many ice cream cones you would've robbed them of)

EVERYONE'S A CRITIC

I swear to GAWD if ONE MORE PERSON who has
"NEVER BEEN ON A STAGE"...
"NEVER BEEN IN THE LIMELIGHT"...
"NEVER PERFORMED LIVE"
"NEVER HAD SOMEONE ASK FOR AN AUTOGRAPH"
shares their opinion about someone who has placed
their souls out to the world for all to see
I'm gonna friggin scream.
SHUT UP!
You don't have the balls to do half of what these
people do on a regular basis... so SHUT UP!
There are 2 type of people in this world...
those who have a life that people love to talk about -
and those who do the talking

Tell me now... which type are you?!

66

JENSON

I was only a half a human
Before you walked through that door
I thought I'd known love
But I hadn't before
You said no words, gave no lines
Just looked me in my eyes
I lost myself that day
Much to my surprise
You are my rock, my foundation
My soul and my heart
You're my passion and privilege
My calm and my spark
You're my everything that matters
My safety in a storm
My reminder to live each day
Like it was the day I was born
You're my husband, my partner
My muse below and above
You are everything I could've never been
My best friend... My love

REAL

It's been years since you left me
For you it's sure been easy
But I see your face in every sad
Experience I have

I like it best when they leave me
I can't love anyone fully
You said I'd never forget you
I never have
I can't love
I can't feel
I can't handle
ANYTHING REAL

It's not bad
But it's not good
You blew your head off
And there I stood
I'm sorry if this makes you shiver
The discomfort it delivers
It may feel bad to you
But it can't get worse for me

I heard him say I'm sorry
I heard him say he loved me
I saw him lift his arm - pull the trigger
Then he left me

I can't love
I can't feel
I can't handle
ANYTHING REAL

It's not bad
But it's not good
He blew his head off
And there I stood

68

DRIFT INTO LOVING REFLECTION

♦

I often sit there & dream of a time when I will have enough letters behind my name, experience, money, success... to where my words will have enough weight to change this world. I realize today, no matter how much I have of the above things, it cannot replace the passion & love I have in my heart.

MAN cannot qualify me to be worthy of respect. My actions, my words & my heart are all the qualifications I need to make this world a better place. As I act my way into a better existence, so shall I show others that it is ok to be loving, vulnerable & happy.

So shall I show others that they are worthy of these things too. So shall I show others that I am the epitome of everything you would tell your children to avoid hanging out with when I was younger, as an adult... those things that I endured, the pain, the suffering, the arrogant thought of myself and the belief that I was owed something by this world, and that I was "the shit"... all of that ickiness has brought me to the woman I am today.

Whether you think I am am worthy of love, respect and kindness is neither here nor there... really... it is what I feel about me, how I treat myself that will pave a way for others to follow suit.

My hope today is that in acknowledging to myself that I am imperfect, and sometimes a little f*cked up, that also I forgive myself for not being everything I and my ego think I should be... the truth is... there have been no mistakes in my life... the good, the bad, the ugly, the indifferent has all brought me to this moment... and in this moment ...

I am ok being "me"... and if you need to hear it today... you are ok being you too... stop judging yourself so harshly... forgive yourself for it all... whatever "it" is... it's over.

Start again... ready................ go.

69

BEAUTIFUL, COURAGEOUS, POWERFUL

Beautiful, courageous, powerful, exotic.

When it all is said and done
Will you stand and be the one?
Embrace your greatness and your truth
You see it all begins with you
And to own it deep inside
The things you once set out to hide
Hand in hand you step right through
To things you never thought you could do

Beautiful, courageous, powerful, exotic.

Playing small and wearing shame
Well that was only just a game
Wasn't a fault to look into
The things that really made you, you
If this whole wide world was blind
One thing certain you would find
What's on the outside is not real
Close your eyes and choose to feel

Beautiful, courageous, powerful, exotic.

70

GPS

There are no greater obstacles in our lives than the ones we can see but truly do not understand. We choose to ignore these obstacles and carry on as though they do not exist. In order to go where our hearts desire to go, we must first pinpoint our starting point.

Once we know and can admit where we truly are at, we can correctly map out a plan of action to go somewhere new, if we so desire. With this in mind, all sorts of new and wonderful experiences and adventures are possible.

IF... THAN... WHO?

IF...
As a free thinking and free acting adult,

I am the one who is making all of my own
choices,
Choosing my own friends,
Writing my own story and choosing the
characters and the scenery...

If I am the one in charge of all of this,
Than who, truly,
Is the Villain of my story?

ADDICTED TO SUFFERING

I became addicted to suffering. Not in a way that made me go out looking for it. I became addicted in a way that I didn't know who I was, or how to live if I wasn't suffering in some way.

I became accustomed to being punished. And if no one was punishing me, I would do it myself.

I did not know how to be okay anymore.

I was born happy, brilliant, without limits in any direction to where I could go. But over the years of my youth I was conditioned and molded into someone I was not born as.

I became... confused. I had no idea what was it felt like to be normal. My normal was not 'normal' anymore.

I felt like I was just existing to exist. This was NOT LIVING, and I was determined to LIVE!

When I say LIVE... I mean flourish, enjoy every moment and embrace this gift of life I was given. But how do I do this?

73

DON'T MISS THE EXPERIENCE

As children, we are born completely "Vulnerable." We are open to everything the world has to offer. When a child falls Victim to an adult's Fears, Lies, or judgments- their ability to remain "Vulnerable" can be affected.

As an adult, we become the one feeding ourselves truths and non-truths. In my scariest adult moments, I have always been faced with the choice of putting up a wall and protecting myself, or the choice of opening up and being "Vulnerable" to the situation in its entirety.

When I have chosen to be "Vulnerable," I have found that I am actually the strongest and the most present. In other words, I don't miss a single part of the experience.

I DIDN'T FORGET

It is so hard to watch you struggle right now with all that you have going on around you.

I know that a part of you feels so alone right now, and that somehow you may have lost your way, but I am here to remind you that you are right on track with your goals.

Just like anyone who sets out to have a new experience, you are facing your challenges. These challenges are all for your greater good. Trust me on this.

You and I also made a pact that if ever you were struggling and couldn't see your way through, I would send a message through human means that would help you move towards the other side.

This poem is that message.

AN UNINSPIRED QUOTE

The life between lives is a most curious thing. Most of the humans on earth don't even remember this time in their conscious minds.

But I know that you have glimpses of these memories.

There are times that you feel this gnawing "knowing" inside you that you can't seem to put your finger on, but it always holds the same feeling for you. "I am meant for more than what I'm doing. There is a purpose and meaning to my life."

These are the things that you say to yourself, but it seems to leave you in confusion. This confusion is fine, but there is a reason you are reading this book right now.

Because your soul yearns to remember the purpose you set for yourself when choosing this lifetime.

Your purpose is tired of waiting and is coming to find you now.   X

I BEGAN TO EXPLAIN

I hadn't seen her in years but it was like we had never lost touch. Only it was as though she didn't know me at all, or so she said.

It has been this way with so many people. Me. The hopeless perpetual victim had become a woman who knows her value and loves herself deeply. I have become the Spiritual Teacher I was born to be and I have evolved into a Spiritual Warrior who helps others to fight their own demons.

She asked, "so what is a Modern Day Spiritual Warrior... and how do I become one?"

She stared at me with curiosity as I contemplated how much I should tell her. Doesn't she know already? I guess not.

So I smiled and I began to explain...

A FULL AND COMPLETE LIFE

The soft colors and sweet voices became the normal routine for the next few months of her life.

As a baby, nothing was expected of her except to eat and sleep. She was good at both of those things.

Eventually she began to understand that there was a routine surrounding everything in her life.

Waking up to the soft colors and brightness of the room, going to sleep to the dull shadows of the same soft colors.

The view of her mothers face brought her a feeling of comfort and safety...

Oh how she yearned to be tightly swaddled up in her arms.

The heartbeat she was so accustomed to hearing beat loud against her ear and lulled her to sleep.

The humming which became familiar to her ears and painted the air with beautiful sounds.

She felt no lack, no emptiness... for the world met her every need.

Day after day, the same routine became week after week, year after year, decade after decade.

The routine changed... her roles shifted and shifted.

Until she was old and great... and her world was overflowing

With knowledge, pain, laughter, joy, love and experiences... oh she had had so many experiences.

Passed down and shared with others.

She had lived a full and wonderful life.

And she was ready... for soon she would lay down for the last time. With her family by her side.

And the soft colors and the sweet voices became the normal routine for the next few days of her life.

Nothing was expected of her except to eat and sleep.

She was good at both things. Up until the moment she left the earth...

And left behind a life completed...

But in her family's hearts... and those that she touched on this earth...

She still lived on forever... for she had lived a full and complete life.

78

HERSTORY

♦

The accounts of the past are flawed.
They were supposed to have been a story of us, and
them and everyone.

As you have demanded before we came here, I will
change the stories into facts which I will present as
"herstory."

You always were funny with words. I may need not
remind you of this - but you said that we have already
heard HIS story - or history as it has been presented,
but this should be a little more accurate than what
we've discussed before.

The writings should have told the truth about why we
are all here and how it all ties in together.

Beware of the tales of HIStory vs. HERstory.

And remember, if either one has been omitted, or one
painted as more important than the other...
Him or Her...The account shall be flawed.

79

YOU ARE DELUSIONAL

Who told you
That you were not
Beautiful - Precious - Perfect

Who told you
That you were
Flawed - Broken - Worthless

Well, fuck them and fuck those delusions
When did you start to believe
That you are not
Beautiful - Precious - Perfect

When did you start owning
That you are
Flawed - Broken - Worthless

These are lies... simply delusions
My sweet reader, If you think you must believe the
things you are told
Believe this
You are perfect... now start owning that instead.

80

HEY LITTLE BOY

♦

Hey little boy
Won't you come here I got something to say
Hey little boy
I got a new game you might wanna play

We can cut my hair
You can cut my skin
We can take it out
But put it back again

I don't think mama likes the noise you play
No... oh no no... little boy... little boy

Hey little boy
With your Vision skateboard
And your Hurley pants on

Hey little boy
I got a new game
You just might wanna
Get your hands on now

You can cut my hair
You can cut my skin

If she takes it out
Just put it back again

I don't think mama likes the noise you play
No... oh no no... little boy... little boy
If we cut my hair
If we cut my skin
If she takes it out
We'll put it back again

Oh no... no no no...

Little boy!

Cut my hair

Cut my hair

Cut my hair

Cut my skin

I don't think mama likes the noise we play!

Hey little boy, won't you come here I got something to say

81

BONNIE & CLYDE

(Co-written with Gene Louis - Gene's lyrics are italicized)

You've got this way of making me smile
And you drive me crazy at every mile
You've got this way of making bad, good
Just ask the ladies, I'm misunderstood
Oh yes you are...

I've got this bad idea
Oh no, you've got this great idea

(together) Let's both play, Bonnie and Clyde
You kill the body and I'll help you hide it
The world is ours, just for tonight
I'll be your Bonnie
And I'll be your Clyde
Just for tonight

If you've got the gun, I've got the ride
You've got that smile, I've got that 'look in my eyes'
I've got this feeling, lucks our best friend
(Together) I've got this feeling..........

(Together) Let's both play, Bonnie and Clyde
You kill the body and I'll help you hide it
The world is ours, just for tonight
I'll be your Bonnie
And I'll be your Clyde
Just for tonight

You know, if they catch us - you should just blame it all
on me
*I'd never do that to you darlin', although it was your
idea*
It kinda was, but I don't think they'll ever be fast
enough to catch us both together
Never, we're like lightning
Lightning in a bottle?
Ha ha, all over the place!
I've got a great idea...
You do have a great idea...

(Together) Let's both play, Bonnie and Clyde
You kill the body and I'll help you hide it
The world is ours, just for tonight
I'll be your Bonnie
Girl, I'll be your Clyde
Just for tonight

Just for tonight...

82

I WANNA ROCK FOR XMAS

♦

So you think you've got what it takes?
Are you my Santa Claus?
Or just the guy who took his place?
We can't find Santa anywhere
And I've been good this year
So please be fair

I'm not asking for too much
But there's some things that should be there

I wanna rock
And I wanna Barbie Mansion
I want a hook that never ends
I hope that this becomes a trend

I wanna rock
And I wanna Barbie Mansion
I wanna play with all my friends
I hope this Christmas never ends

I saw Santa yesterday
I was on his lap
And he was in his sleigh
With a smile he said to me
You've been good this year

So what do you want from me?

I'm not asking for too much
But there's some things that should be there

I wanna rock
And I wanna Barbie Mansion
I want a hook that never ends
I hope that this becomes a trend

I wanna rock
And I wanna Barbie Mansion
I wanna play with all my friends
I hope this Christmas never ends

Grab the reins and come with me
Let's hang some Christmas lights
And decorate the tree

Grab the reins and come with me....

Cause I wanna rock
And I wanna Barbie Mansion
I want a hook that never ends
I hope that this becomes a trend

I wanna rock
And I wanna Barbie Mansion
I wanna play with all my friends
I hope this Christmas never ends

THE JUNEBUG IS MY BOSS

She is wise beyond years
She is funny and brave
She laughs at my jokes
And she gets them, I think
She reminds me to be polite
She's the boss of me, you see
She tells me stories of adventures
Not knowing she's one herself
She is grateful and beautiful
She's a source of timelessness
For I am Grandma to her
Or Babushka, if you please
She has brought inquisitiveness
And my surrender
She has changed my world completely
I would do anything she asks
No matter what it may be
I'm her slave, she has conquered
She is the air that I breathe
Yes the Junebugs mind
Is a mysterious thing
She's my boss, I'm just her subject
What would you like? Anything!

✗

83

A SCRIPT IN A WEEKEND

I always have wondered what it's like in your mind
You have darkness so beautiful, yet you show up so kind
You are quick to add honesty with your tongue in your cheek
LA to New York - of Salt Lake City - do we speak?
Inspiration you gave me, the way you opened your soul
Your unapologetic banter & general refusal to play a role
The fucking coolest person I'd ever met, that was you -
You my friend -
And your creations are legendary
From beginning to end
When you tell stories I'm in the middle, I'm their ears, I'm their eyes
Angry and defiant - I feel their sadness and their cries
You are talented, and magical and weird and so real
You're a perfect mix of human... that's how I feel.

I felt this one was a perfect closer. I wrote it a few years back.

82

I WISH

I wish I didn't feel the way that I feel
I wish I didn't get so angry with everything that you do
I "think" that you love me but I'm honestly not sure
I wish we could start over - but even then, you never really did like me - did you?

These aren't my words either. They are yours. And I am so confused. All I have ever wanted was to be loved by you. To be good enough without it being anything about you. Just an authentic relationship. Without weird rules and behavioral protocols. I just wanted one time in my life for you to look at me and be proud of me instead of jealous. Just let me have a moment in the sunshine without having to dim my light when it comes to you. I want to NOT be afraid of you emotionally.

I know you know that I love you. I know you know this. But I'm afraid I will never be safe when it comes to you. And that's just not fair at all. It's not what I want. But it is what it is. And I'm angry. I really am. Disappointed and angry. I feel like I got robbed of your love. I feel like it should've been safe for us to love each other. But I'm still here. And I'm willing to let it be different. We have time. As long as we're both here. We have time. ✗

83

DADDY'S LITTLE GIRL

🌢

Yep. Judge me if you will. I am daddy's little girl. How could I not be? If you know him then you know how much he loves me. From the day I took my first breath, and every moment since - I have known that I was the center of his Universe. I have known how precious I am to him. I don't have to compete for his love with anyone else, ever. He loves all that he loves with all of his heart. And none of us feel like it's a competition. It's just the way he is. Always honest, always straight forward and every time he speaks, he speaks with absolutely love. I am my daddy's little girl. I've been his biggest fan since I was a child watching him stand on stage and play his guitar for the crowds, I wanted to be him. I wanted to be just - like - him.

And I was. In so many more ways than were probably considered a good thing. And when I hit the same roadblocks he hit - he guided me through them. Without shame, guilt judgment or owing him a damned thing. He taught me so much. But I think the best thing I learned from him was how to make a child feel unconditionally loved. I'm not sure I did it anywhere near as well as he does. But I did my best. And one thing he always says is. . . "As long as you did your best, it's good enough for me." ✗

Final Words

Honestly, seriously and without any hesitation I offer these final words to you in this book.

Don't ever...and I mean EVER let someone else tell you who you are. Or how you should feel. Be you. As long as you are acting in integrity and not doing anything unethical, illegal or immoral - do what you want without hesitation, reservation, guilt or shame. This life is too short to be held down by prejudice, opinions or the rules that others have made for themselves. Be a good person, bring only love to everything you do. Fuck the haters, fuck the shamers, fuck those who try to demand that you live lift by their rules, morals and values.

FIGURE OUT WHAT IT TRULY MEANS TO BE YOU.

AND BE THAT.

If I had believed all of the things that people told me about myself over the years, I would never have been able to accomplish all that I've done in my life. I would never know what true vulnerability or true strength looks and feels like. I would've lost out on so much life and living.

If you need permission to be you, I am not going to do that for you. Because no one has truly ever taken that permission from you. Hold that head up high!
You're awesome... own it.

ABOUT THE AUTHOR

Franki is a lyricist, poet, entertainer, philosopher, teacher, human, mother, wife and grandmother. In her recovery from pain, abuse and addiction, Franki Olinger has inspired others to understand, love & accept themselves vulnerably and authentically. In this new book, "The Softness Under The Scars: A Collection of Private and Not So Private Lyrics, Poems & Thoughts", Franki has bravely decided to share some of her deepest as well as darkest works with others, with the message that there is darkness & light that blends together in every human being. Raw and unedited words about her boyfriend shooting himself in front of her, childhood abuse and loss. As well as uplifting, encouraging and spiritual thoughts. Franki brings pure authenticity to each and every page. If you are a lover of honest and vulnerable rawness, this book will be a page turner for you.

Made in the USA
Coppell, TX
28 December 2021

70107748R00085